THE PORTAGE POETRY SERIES

SERIES TITLES

Forgive the Animal
Sarah Pape

Love as Invasive Species
Ellen Kombiyil

They Were Horrible Cooks
Allison Whittenberg

The New Life
Wendy Wisner

Restoring Prairie
Margaret Rozga

Table with Burning Candle
Julia Paul

A Bright Wound
Sarah A. Etlinger

The Velvet Book
Rae Gouirand

Listening to Mars
Sally Ashton

Glitter City
Bonnie Jill Emanuel

The Trouble with Being a Childless Only Child
Michelle Meyer

Happy Everything
Caitlin Cowan

Dear Lo
Brady Bove

Sadness of the Apex Predator
Dion O'Reilly

Do Not Feed the Animal
Hikari Miya

The Watching Sky
Judy Brackett Crowe

Let It Be Told in a Single Breath
Russell Thorburn

The Blue Divide
Linda Nemec Foster

Lake, River, Mountain
Mark B. Hamilton

Talking Diamonds
Linda Nemec Foster

Poetic People Power
Tara Bracco (ed.)

The Green Vault Heist
David Salner

There is a Corner of Someplace Else
Camden Michael Jones

Everything Waits
Jonathan Graham

We Are Reckless
Christy Prahl

Always a Body
Molly Fuller

Bowed As If Laden With Snow
Megan Wildhood

Silent Letter
Gail Hanlon

Dining on Salt

"The eighty septets in *Dining on Salt* capture tender care for an ill spouse and her subsequent death. These are lines of grief and going on. Rather than feeling contained, each septet has space enough to widen into understanding."

—LAUREN CAMP
New Mexico Poet Laureate
author of *In Old Sky*

"Wayne Lee's stunning and original new work, *Dining on Salt: Four Seasons of Septets*, is a full-length exploration of loss, using the septet poem (seven lines, including examples of twenty traditional septet forms) as a channel to his inspiration. The book begins with meditations on nature, companionship, aging and the environment, but abruptly becomes a memoir in verse about his wife's sudden death. These are short exhalations of grief, but also of timelessness and beauty. He generously allows his words to evolve into a broader lament for the planet: birds become totems of consolation and connection. He writes from the edge of a koi pond: *Some grief must be drowned in small words and soft sounds.* Yet these evocative and insightful septets aren't just gestures of bereavement, but ruminations on an uncertain future with its mutable landscapes and sudden joys. At their best, his poems reveal how each of us is born one loss at a time."

—JOHN MACKER
author of *Desert Threnody*

"Wayne Lee's *Dining on Salt* is a powerful collection of elegiac, lyric septets. The poems map a journey through caregiving, loss, healing and renewal: *such a small task, so brief the work / to inhale the scent of the world / to savor it and let it go....* Potent with the concision and directness of haiku, Lee's seven-line form is also expansive enough to carry the weight of grief. His moving tribute to his late wife shows us a way of moving forward, day by day, poem by poem, toward healing, toward "a window thrown open / all the world blowing through."

—ALICIA HOKANSON
author of *Perishable World*

"Stepping into Wayne Lee's septets offers a breath of living. Any loss, regret or grief becomes a burnished gold."

—HIRAM LAREW
author of *This Very Much*

"One of the remarkable septets in *Dining on Salt* opens on a simple moment: *We share this quiet morning space / in peace, the sleeping cat and I.* Images of morning light follow—*the cobalt vase, / the purple buds that look a bit like / lilacs, my blue-veined hand*—and then this: *All I ask is to see, / to breathe inside this mystery.* Here, in eighty poems of seven lines each, Wayne Lee's request is granted. He sees into the mystery of grief and the heartbreak of loss, and shares these shimmering moments with us."

—DAVID MEISCHEN
author of *Caliche Road Poems*

Dining on Salt

Four Seasons of Septets

Wayne Lee

CORNERSTONE PRESS
UNIVERSITY OF WISCONSIN-STEVENS POINT

Cornerstone Press, Stevens Point, Wisconsin 54481
Copyright © 2025 Wayne Lee
www.uwsp.edu/cornerstone

Printed in the United States of America by
Point Print and Design Studio, Stevens Point, Wisconsin

Library of Congress Control Number: 2025932493
ISBN: 978-1-960329-85-1

Cornerstone Press titles are produced in courses and internships offered by the
Department of English at the University of Wisconsin–Stevens Point.

DIRECTOR & PUBLISHER
Dr. Ross K. Tangedal

EXECUTIVE EDITORS
Jeff Snowbarger, Freesia McKee

EDITORIAL DIRECTOR
Brett Hill

SENIOR EDITOR
Ellie Atkinson

PRESS STAFF
Samantha Bjork, Sophie McPherson, Ava Willett, Madison Schultz, Paige Biever,
Lillian Kulbeck, Autumn Vine, Allison Lange

—for Alice

ALSO BY WAYNE LEE:

Buddha's Cat: Poems

Googling a Present Participle: Poems, Prose Poems, Bogus Monologues & Fraudulent Artifacts

The Underside of Light

Twenty Poems from the Blue House

CONTENTS

I. That Sounding Sense

II. This One Sock

III. Whiter than the Palest Skin

IV. Gestures of Preservation

PREFACE

Four Seasons of Septets

An old poet friend commemorated his 60th birthday by publishing a chapbook of sestets, six-line poems. I liked the idea, so in 2018, when I started my 70th year on this planet, I decided to write a collection of septets, seven-line poems. I took my friend's idea a couple steps further, though, by imposing upon myself the Draconian discipline of writing *nothing but septets* for the entire year. I also resolved to average at least one septet a day during that time. I came up a bit shy of that last goal, but I did resist the temptation to write anything longer or shorter than seven lines.

When I started my septetathon, there was no way I could have foreseen what a dramatic—and traumatic—twelve months it would prove to be. Some things were knowns. I had been the caregiver for my disabled wife for many years, and I was burned out. Alice had a terminal, genetic, neurological condition called spinocerebellar ataxia type 3, and her health had deteriorated to the point where we had to put her in an assisted living facility in Portland, Oregon. I was renting a room in a farmhouse 23 miles away, driving back and forth to care for her. It had been a long, exhausting ordeal watching my life partner lose so many of her gifts and abilities. Still, I thought we had at least a few more years together.

Then, one afternoon three months into my project, the unknown—and unthinkable—happened when Alice swallowed enough pills to end her life, without telling me.

I spent the next nine months trying to cope with the shock of that loss, stumbling through my grieving process and doing my best to recreate my life as a widower. I celebrated Alice at two memorials in Portland and one in Santa Fe, where we had previously lived. While I was in New Mexico, I fell in love with the Land of Enchantment all over again, so I moved back and started over.

It was a lot to cope with. Capturing the upheaval of that year in seven-line capsules was a daunting challenge. But my writing practice has always been a way for me to process life experiences, so in the end I was grateful for my self-imposed discipline. The limitations of the seven-line forms forced me to crystalize my thoughts and feelings and helped me digest them in bite-sized bits, rather than choking on the enormity of it all.

It didn't take long before I became enamored of the power and potential of the many septet variations. Their compact size struck a balance between the mini-satori of the haiku and the classical architecture of the sonnet. I didn't have any models for how to go about composing a heptastich (HEP-tuh-stick), so I just set out on my own. At first I wrote all my drafts in free verse. Then I began researching traditional, seven-line forms to see how other writers had worked with them. I discovered a rich body of literature dating back more than 800 years. It started with Chaucer, who invented the rime (or rhyme) royal, the mother of all English-language heptastichs. I found dozens of different seven-line inventions, both historic and contemporary, with enticing names like rondelet, lyrette, saraband, seguidilla, diamante, Sicilian septet, star sevlin, Pleiades and Kwansaba. I learned that seven-line forms, though not in vogue these days, are still being created. In fact, there has been a modest renaissance in recent years, with some writers inventing their own new forms to add to the canon.

A word of clarification: "septet" has two different poetic meanings. The narrow definition is a free-verse, seven-line poetic form that follows an *aabbccx* rhyme scheme. The term also refers more broadly to any seven-member group, grouping, object, formation or entity that is considered a single unit, including a seven-line stanza or poem. All seven-line poems are heptastichs, with their own specific requirements. Since "heptastich" is a largely unfamiliar term, I use "septet" both ways in this book—for the specific *aabbccx* form and as a synonym for any and all seven-line poems.

As I unearthed more and more traditional forms, I began experimenting with some of them. I was struck by the power and potential that seven lines afford, and I gained great respect for the precision and restraint required to work within their tight strictures. Among my 80 poems included in this collection are examples of 20 of the 40 traditional and contemporary forms I identified.

If Shakespeare had built his sonnets as *duodoras,* using two septets instead of three quatrains and a couplet, perhaps heptastichs would have remained as popular as sonnets, villanelles, pantoums, sestinas, limericks and other line-count forms. It is my hope that this collection might reinvigorate interest in this dynamic, concise family of poetic forms. May it inspire other poets to try their hand at the many inviting variations, and maybe even create their own new ones.

—W.L.

I.

That Sounding Sense

Mirage

From the back seat, I stared in wonder
as the water disappeared from the road
before our car could plow through it.

How does it feel to face my eighth
decade on this shimmering pearl?
I've learned to close my eyes and trust
that there's always more than we can see.

What a Wonderful World

I hold your waist as you transfer from wheelchair
to toilet seat, pull down your wet pullup
and pajama bottom, replace them
with a dry diaper and clean cotton pants.

We stand like that for one sweet moment,
your forehead pressed against my chest,
swaying to that first slow dance in the park.

A Word from Grandmother

Each day on my forest walk I pause
to press my palms against her skin,
the wrinkles on the backs of my hands
miniatures of her great ridges and ravines.

Each day I wait like that until she speaks,
blesses me with a single-word benediction.

Yesterday it was *peace*. Today it is *patience*.

Kumbhaka

(Sanskrit for "the retention of the breath
in the hatha yoga practice of pranayama")

In that scant pause between breaths,
after you push the air from your lungs
and before you pull it in again—
that is when the miracle occurs.

We die so many deaths on our path, but
always we are reborn. I spent a billion years
in the bardo learning to turn stone to flesh.

What Lies Within: A Spanish Septet

Before I open my eyes, I peer
into hers to see if I can share
her dream. Deep inside the Earth
a gemstone glistens on a moonless night.
Beneath the waves, a blind fish finds
its way. In the darkness we merge
and what we cannot see disappears.

A Bit Like Lilacs: A Rime Royal

We share this quiet morning space
in peace, the sleeping cat and I.
Sunlight catches the cobalt vase,

the purple buds that look a bit like
lilacs, my blue-veined hand that writes

these lines. All I ask is to see,
to breathe inside this mystery.

Gondola

Some days I am no age at all
in a world outside of time,

like I'm floating in a hot air balloon,
feeling no wind because I'm moving
with the wind.

I kiss the ground with no idea
where I've been.

Reading to My Wife

Will you read to me? she asks
when she can't sleep. Will you read
from *Peter Rabbit* or *Winnie the Pooh*?

So I sit by her bed rail and narrate again
the tales she knows so well, until the meds
kick in, until she closes her eyes,
clutching her favorite bear.

Hall of Mirrors

There are two ways of spreading light:
to be the candle or the mirror that reflects it.
—Edith Wharton

You are not just the moon, my love.
Each of us is moon and sun
in this hall of mirrors.

What does it matter who is seer and who
is seen, so long as there is sight?

That kiss you gave me this morning?
It's the same one I gave you last night.

Spores

How far can a spore travel?

I make myself light as fluff, drift
through day and night

in your direction, but
so much depends upon the wind.

The destination is so distant
and I am but a single cell.

Teacup: A Septet II

If kissing
scars is wisdom, then
I earned the one on my heart
by climbing the sky and tumbling back
to Earth. A teacup shatters
on stone tiles and gets
filled with tea.

Because one million species are in danger of extinction

I use a reused baggie to wrap my organic free-range chicken salad sandwich on gluten-free quinoa-amaranth-flax-seed bread and pack it with an organic non-GMO apple and a gluten- and dairy-free organic almond butter cookie in a post-consumer recycled paper bag and take along a thermos of fair-trade decaf coffee with raw honey and organic soy milk—and still I hold a ticking time bomb to the head of the last surviving giraffe.

Clearcut

All I own is an ax and all the world
is old growth and all the owls pivot
their heads to look and all their eggs
are memories of refuge. They forget
the gophers and voles that squirmed
in their talons and all the live young
that once wriggled under the ground.

Wildfires

The sky is choked with smoke
as the green lungs of the Earth turn

black. In this middle world we burn
in the wildfires of consumption.

We are both fuel and flame,
seasoned wood and healing rain.

We drink before we drown.

Minor Deities

The ant prays to the beetle and the aphid.

Do you doubt that trees communicate
through their roots like lovers
touching toes under the restaurant table?

We all sit on someone's altar
and on someone else's dinner plate.

We're all aflame in this fight against fire.

Hot: A Sept

Hot—
no wind
to speak of,
so I won't speak.
I listen
for moth
wings.

Whistling

—for Jean Merrilyn Rood (1922–2016)

I heard a bird today that sounded like my mother,
the way she whistled when she thought no one
was listening. She could have been a goldfinch
or a varied thrush calling from across a field.

It's balmy today, a calm breeze brushing past
evergreens, the way voices carry downwind,
how you can hear what you cannot see.

A Walk with My Mother

We fall into an easy rhythm, she and I, strolling
slowly enough to notice which wildflowers
are in bloom, which songbirds are mating,
which neighbors have put in wheat.
I tell her what new words the girls have learned,
what the latest CAT scan means for my wife.
Mom sighs and says she misses life on Earth.

An Elder Addresses His Pain: A Sicilian Septet

At this late stage of life
pain is a bad old friend
and each worn bone in my spine
a broken agreement.

I believe in compromise,
so here's the deal: I'll pretend
to be brave, you appear to be kind.

Watching Koi: A Flint

The ancient one floats almost slack
in the flow, poses, gives me time

to consider the saffron of her brow
and abundance of her lashes,

the silken embroidery of her broad back
and fins trailing like horsetail clouds.

Each of us is reflected in the sky.

The Bat

She yells at the walls of her small apartment,
the ceiling, window, door. She feels trapped
in her assisted living cell, she says, shut off
from the life she lived, the world she loved.

Once a bat got in her room and flapped in frantic
circles, desperate to escape. Oh, to have that
sounding sense, to find one's way free again.

Seller of Birds

On the last day of his life, the seller of birds
unlatched the doors to all the bamboo cages
in his shop, freed each of his finches, parakeets
and cockatiels, then lay on his cot to die.

One old parrot refused to leave, crouched
on his perch, stared at his mirror, rocked
and squawked *pretty boy, pretty boy, pretty boy.*

Three-Legged Dog

More and more parts of her go missing.

She asks if I would rather lose my mind,
like her mother, or my body, like her.
I answer I'd rather not lose my wife.

There's just so much a man can take. Or give.

I watch a three-legged dog chase a ball
and wait for the phantom limb to land.

II.

This One Sock

Flying

Just as I'm missing the birds
that have flown from the cold
and the yellow leaves twisting
in the wind, I meet a girl of five
or six skipping down the street,
arms outstretched, hair blown wild,
flying in her heart.

Sunlight: A Shanzi

—for Alice Rose Lee (1952–2018)

My wife takes her
life and an angel
suddenly appears.
I kiss her, then
she too flies off.
Blinding sunlight,
then the darkest night.

Master Gardener

Rose is the name she gave herself,
heirloom roses what she painted,
what she planted and tended
wherever she lived.

On my altar, long green stems,
red petals scattered
all around.

Dining on Salt: A Whitney

No dinner,
again. Empty
heart, empty
belly. Dining
on salt, on
all that is left
after the sea has dried up.

The widower wakes to a cold room,

misses her back against his,
waits for the sun to burn through
the gloom. Still in his unwashed pjs,
he wills himself to pull on socks
and make a pot of coffee.
With no appetite for oatmeal or eggs,
he crawls back into an unmade bed.

Grown Man Sleeps with Stuffed Puppy

His name is Barnaby. He is very, very old.
He has sad, brown eyes and wears a scarf
around his neck like Alice wore.

She took him everywhere she went, slept
with him every night until the very end.

I hold him close—
inhale a hint of her face creme.

Apricots

The sweet reek of apricots
rotting on the ground,

the ache for all that is fallen
and gone to waste,

dry toast growing cold
on his plate

as he stares at her chair.

Heaven

I went walking the day after my wife died,
asked a passing stranger if he would pray for her.
He did, then started in on me. The next morning
he stopped by my house unannounced, offered
me a Bible with special passages marked in red
and left a tract in my mailbox that explained
in detail exactly what it takes to get into Heaven.

More Wine: An Alliterisen

Too much pain today. Too much
wine. Or maybe not enough.

When a tall tree falls and dies,
its crown clears space in the sky.

The things we lose. The lovers,
the lives that don't recover from life.

More wine, please. Much more.

White Dog

A white dog would lie
on her grave
and moan

if she had a grave.

I sit at the valley door
and wait for her
to call my name.

Her Cat

I worry about Rosa since Alice died.

When my business failed we lost
our house, but we moved on, rebuilt
our lives, made it work however
we could, wherever we were.

This is not like that, though, this loss.
There is no home for this old cat.

A Voice

I don't know how anymore,
says the man who shared his bed
with a voice—how to eat,
how to sleep, how to breathe.

But one day he changes the sheets,
opens the windows and doors.

The dog snores just like his wife.

Friend

My Down's friend Jon asks
How's your friend Alice doing?

She died, I say.
That's nice, says Jon.

Alice is my wife, I say louder.
Jon pauses. *How's your friend Alice?*

She's fine, I say. *Just fine.*

Hard Freeze

Time to bring in the geraniums and coleus,
to cover the roses, peppers and kale,
to wrap the faucets and pipes.

It's the icy chill that kills the wool-
gathered summer, the shocking slap
on the cheek that drags us back.

I can't remember when it was warm.

Mateless

I don't know what to do with this one sock,
this solitary blue-and-pink thing with a hole
in the toe, the one that still smells like her foot.

How do you toss away the last remaining trace
of someone you love, the fleeting, the ephemeral,
the evanescence that lingers
like perfume…

Sense of Smell

Such a small task, so brief the work
to inhale the scent of the world,
to savor it and let it go, to trust
that you will have the chance again
to taste the succulence and decay,
the plums and peaches rotting in the grass,
the steaming dish of apple crisp.

Her Brushes, Her Pens, Her

Her brushes, her pens, her ink.
Her paper, scissors, stone.
Her gluestick, masking tape, mask.
Her easel, paint-stained hands, pain.
Her roses, sunsets, ghostly trees.
Her painterliness, out of bounds, out of time.
Her date. Her frame. Her chop. Her name.

III.

Whiter than the Palest Skin

Root Soup

I have this hunger for rootstocks, for rutabagas
and Yukon Gold potatoes, for unpeeled carrots, turnips,
parsnips, for the fruits of the Earth that ripen slowly
in the autumn sun, for sweet onion, plump garlic,
skin-on delicata squash. And for the kiss of seasoning,
for sea salt, rosemary, peppercorns, lemon thyme.
I have this need for what lies beneath.

Windowpane

Ice on the pond
thin as a windowpane.

Some grief must be drowned
in small words and soft sounds.

Koi slow themselves down in winter,
grow so cold they eat no food at all.

Clouds float below my feet.

Diminished Chords

—after Maurice Ravel's "String Quartet in F minor"

You know about love, you who have played
the diminished chords of longing and loss.
Forever the music of beauty beckons
like something glimpsed at the edge
of the glade, tempting you beyond safety
and warmth, you who are so beautifully
unresolved.

Spoons

Once again, this day dawns without my love.
Gone are the kisses on rising, kisses
on drifting off as one, soft spoons
through the night. No more backrubs in bed,
no afternoon naps in which we do not nap
at all. And then there's tomorrow,
a day that never ends…

Arithmetic

The sum of who we are is love.

Such a grand answer from a man
who can't remember what he had

for breakfast. There's arithmetic
in every kiss, every ecstasy, every letting go.

Ask me your question again
once I have left the Earth.

Infrared: A Pleiades

If something is warm,
it is necessarily bright.

In the deep night
I feel your glow.

I know you are gone, but
it is not a dream, this vision
in the heat of my sleep.

Melting

Snow this morning, ragged tufts
against a flat, gray sky.

When my wife died, I thought I,
too, would perish from the cold.

I glance down—
a single snowflake melts
as it touches the ground.

Sight

A Steller's jay lights in the Indian plum,
bright blue against the dull brown
of twisted branches and limbs.

Snow below on fallen leaves, pale sky
above a green fringe of cedar and fir.

How much we miss, we who have sight,
we who long to close our eyes.

Widower

After she died, I cared for myself
as mammals care: by licking my fur.
I lay across my wife's cold form like a dog
guarding a newly sodded mound, moaned
and mourned there as orphans moan
and mourn. Then came the howling night,
the wandering off, lost, alone.

Echo Amphitheater

I wait in the snow for my voice
to return, my solo baritone that throws
her name against the curved stone shell,

but when the sound rebounds
it is a whisper, not a cry, a broken alto
mouthing my name, not hers.

Again I call, but she is gone.

This Bowl

I'll keep this bowl, this one
remaining dish from a set
of two because it is broken,
because she dropped it,
because in her condition
she dropped lots of things.
I wonder what can be repaired.

Accident: A Septolet

Yesterday
I accidentally
threw out
your old love
letters.

You, who died
on me.

Navigator

That rattle in the armrest? My wife's red lipstick.
Those one-armed glasses in the glovebox? Hers.
That torn map, that stale donut under the seat,
that tin angel hanging from the rearview mirror?
Hers, all hers.

That driver, red-eyed, road-weary, lost?
Hers, until she tells me where to turn.

Infinitive

Ghost is a verb,
as in *to spirit away.*

When she unbodied,
embrace became *empty,*
feast became *starve.*

The air is thick with dust,
the wind invisible.

Little Brown Birds

All these leaves on the ground,
all these different trees—
I didn't know until she showed me—

and all these little brown birds
that flit away so fast—
I didn't know their names,
would not have known if not for her.

Strength

I've grown weak since she's been gone—arms,
shoulders, back—all those parts that worked
so hard each day to load and unload her chair,
to lift, lower and carry, to help her sit, stand
and ambulate, to hold her close in hopes
she wouldn't fall again. All those parts of me
she helped make strong—hands, hips, heart.

Healthy Choices

I'm off chocolate now. It was either that or give up wine.
I consulted the *I-Ching*. It said a goat gets its horns stuck in a hedge.
I stopped watching boxing and started reading about tai chi.
I switched to whole wheat pizza.
My horoscope said I'm on the cusp of making new friends.
I walk to Baskin-Robbins now. You'd be proud of me,
the way I've learned to cough into my elbow.

Survivor

I loved that birch, her graceful curve, bowed
earthward from the blizzard of ninety-six.
I saw a kind of courage in her work to lift
her crown again toward the canopy.

Now I grieve the empty space she filled,
the mound of fresh-cut rounds on the ground,
her bark whiter than the palest skin.

IV.

Gestures of Preservation

A Sudden Passing: A Spanish Saraband

First clear day of spring.
I look again and it's gone.
This is about seeing,

not losing sight.
I'm blinded by sunbeams,
then suddenly it's night.
Her face appears in dreams.

Life List: A Sevenling

Three redtail hawks circle high above
the tallest hemlock, hover on updrafts
over the creek, then one flies off alone.

I still have the *Peterson Field Guide*
she gave me for Christmas, my notes
in the margins, my life list incomplete.

Who will verify my sightings?

Things with Feathers

Once again the redtails revisit the nest
they built three years ago in the cedar tree.

Two Junes in a row they've flown away
with no fledglings to show for their devotion.
But now, again, they fetch new sticks and twigs

to weave among the old. Hope is indeed the thing
with feathers, the spring that holds no memory of snow.

Spring, again

Famine in Yemen, gunmen in New Zealand,
catastrophic flooding across the Great Plains.

Spring is a promise, not a guarantee.
The planet shifts on its axis, a wobbling top,

and every day we must learn to stand and walk
again, watching for falling planes overhead,
the first green shoots of crocus underfoot.

The Keening

Think of pain as a caged animal.
Think of desire as a lost limb.

There is a marsh where red-winged blackbirds congregate
like pilgrims, their strange harmonic whistling a wail for all
the nests they've left behind, for those they've yet to weave.

Be like that, freed from your past, keening
for the great murmuration.

Dragonfly: A Lyrette

Sapphire
dragonfly
circles me twice,
but doesn't dare land
on my hand. She
said she would
visit.

Leafing

The Indian plum is the first to leaf, as usual.
Rufous-sided towhees and dark-eyed juncos
scratch in the mulch for seed, starlings
and Western bluebirds compete for nesting boxes,
redtail hawks rule the highest cedar bough.

I rise from my narrow bed, from memories
of ice, to face a world somehow turning green.

Sixteenth Day of Spring: A Septorale

Three mule deer venture out at dusk,
leave the Doug fir underbrush and munch
on sweet, young, meadow grass.

Alert to each new threat, their ears pivot
and tails twitch in gestures of preservation.

Let me be the first to bless the feast, and
taste each bite as though it were my last.

On Listening to "The Lark Ascending"

—after the single-movement work by Ralph Vaughn Williams

Barn swallows swoop through morning mist,
house wrens flit from post to nest,
a kestrel passes soundlessly overhead.

There are no larks here, though, ascending
or otherwise. We take what we are given
and make do with what we have, attuned
to something beyond what we can hear.

The Lark Ascended

—for Mica and Annie

It's their first Mother's Day without their mom
and they are pulled in two, toward the open arms
of their thirsty girls and that vast expanse of sky.

Flute song on the radio, rising like prayer.

Once there was a lark, and speckled eggs,
and fledglings testing their wings. Now they flutter
upward like that most ephemeral of melodies.

Esme

The branches of the pear tree are studded
with plump, white buds, even as some
of last year's crop still hang like sleeping bats.

Yesterday we scattered her grandma's ashes
in the outbound tide; today Esme plays
with her blocks, builds a wall, knocks it down.

Each of us is born one loss at a time.

Snakeskin: A Septet

I found a garter snakeskin
in the overrun garden,
translucent as a scrim.
It must have taken some time
for the creature to inhabit
its new self, learning to live
in a world it has outgrown.

Fuel for the Fire: A Pleiades

If your thought is a rose, you are a rose garden;
and if it is a thistle, you are fuel for the fire.
       —Rumi

The house finches fight over
thistle seed at the feeder
that I hung three days ago on
the backyard fence.

They don't need me, but I need
them to show me how not
to burn.

Window

I am not the empty room,
the stale air, the sealed memory.

Nor am I the scent of spring,
the fragrant breath of rebirth.

I stand somewhere in between—
a window thrown open,
all the world blowing through.

The Days: A Pyramid

So much to say in one life-
time, with the clock ticking
down and time itself
growing quiet
until it, too,
becomes
mute.

Hinge: A Rime Royal

My door was half a bubble out of plumb,
hung like a rucksack with just one strap.
All it needed was a new hinge, a shim
and some elbow grease to screw it back.
I twisted the knob and opened it a crack
to face a forest of weeds. No doubt
the world wanted in like I wanted out.

Green Plums

Spring is when we eat things that are not yet done,
says my young Israeli friend. *Green fava beans,*
raw green peas, green plums—for us
they are not unripe, they are just right.
So I pluck a sour plum from the tree and try it
with a pinch of salt, as he suggests. *Not bad,* I say,
but I think I'll wait until it turns to wine.

Helicopters: A Sept

I'm
searching
for meaning
today. Meanwhile
winged seeds spin
toward
Earth.

Wild Goose

The Canada geese flap north in formation, then one peels off and veers south. I worry about that goose, how it will fend, where it might end up.

We're all flock animals. We need one another. We're all made of air.

There is a land where nests are woven from flesh, where eggshells crack and life pecks its way blindly out of the darkness.

If you get lost, I'll find you. If we get lost, it will be for love.

Knife and Plate: A Septet

We trade words
like hand-made goods
at a great bazaar. I call
your knife beautiful,
you admire my plate.
Come, let us break
the bread of understanding.

Cradle of Bones

The world we sit on
is one long curve.

Let the wind rock you
like a cradle of bones
so you may know how it feels

to sleep in the treetops
while never leaving the Earth.

Seeds: A Cameo

We merge
as a prayer within
each other, ask for what we need.

We are seeds
becoming trees becoming seeds.

Sing to me while you still have
the words.

Appendices

A BRIEF HISTORY
OF THE SEPTET

The first known appearance of a heptastich (seven-line poem) in English was in the late 13th century when Geoffrey Chaucer (c.1340s-1400) used the form in his 8,239-line epic poem "Troilus and Criseyde." Each stanza of the poem consists of seven iambic pentameter lines rhyming *ababbcc*. Here is the first stanza:

> The double sorwe of Troilus to tellen,
> That was the king Priamus sone of Troye,
> In lovinge, how his aventures fellen
> Fro wo to wele, and after out of Ioye,
> My purpos is, er that I parte fro ye.
> Thesiphone, thou help me for tendyte
> Thise woful vers, that wepen as I wryte!

Chaucer also employed the form in five of his "Canterbury Tales."

He didn't invent the rime royal, though. Chaucer was influenced by earlier Italian writers such as Guillaume de Machaut (c. 1300-1377) and Giovanni Boccaccio (1313-1375), who were already writing septets. "Troilus" was, in fact, based on Boccaccio's "Il Filostrato," a narrative poem written in ottava rima, an eight-line form. French writers had been using the seven-line rime royal form since the 13th century, which they called chant royale. They preferred it for ceremonies, especially those celebrating the arrival of royals into cities, as well as for mock ceremonies at guild festivals.

Chaucer himself never referred to the form as rime royal. That term was believed to have been coined by Chaucer admirer King James I of Scotland (1394-1437), who took up the form, which he called rhyme royale, in his collection of romantic poems *The Kingis Quair* (*The King's Book*). The form also became known as the Chaucerian stanza and Troilus stanza.

Rime royal became a preferred stanzaic form for long narrative poems during the 15th and early 16th centuries. Poet and critic George Gascoigne (c. 1535-1577) explained that, "This hath bene called Rithme royall, and surely it is a royall kinde of verse, serving best for grave discourses." Sir Thomas Wyatt (1503–1542) wrote his poem, "They Flee from Me," in five rime royal stanzas. Here is stanza number one:

> They flee from me that sometime did me seek
> With naked foot, stalking in my chamber.
> I have seen them gentle, tame, and meek,
> That now are wild and do not remember
> That sometime they put themself in danger
> To take bread at my hand; and now they range,
> Busily seeking with a continual change.

Wyatt later took more liberties with the form in his "A Revocation," using an *ababacc* rhyme scheme and a then-radical use of dimeter syllabic count. It opens this way:

> What should I say?
> —Since Faith is dead,
> And Truth away
> From you is fled?
> Should I be led

With doubleness?
Nay! nay! mistress.

Sir Edmund Spenser (c. 1552-3-1599) made his contribution with the irregularly metered "Fowre Hymnes," which departs from pentameter to alexandrine (12 iambic syllables) in L6. Here is the opening stanza:

Loue, that long since hast to thy mighty powre,
Perforce subdude my poore captiued hart,
And raging now therein with restlesse stowre,
Doest tyrannize in euerie weaker part;
Faine would I seeke to ease my bitter smart,
By any seruice I might do to thee, Or ought
that else might to thee pleasing bee.

William Shakespeare (1565-1616) also tried his hand at the form. He arranged the 1,855 iambic pentameter lines of his epic poem "The Rape of Lucrece" in the traditional rime royal format, although it did not meet with much success. Here is the first of his 265 stanzas:

From the besieged Ardea all in post,
Borne by the trustless wings of false desire,
Lust-breathed Tarquin leaves the Roman host,
And to Collatium bears the lightless fire
Which, in pale embers hid, lurks to aspire
And girdle with embracing flames the waist
Of Collatine's fair love, Lucrece the chaste.

John Milton (1608-1674) published his "On the Morning of Christ's Nativity" in 1645 in his *Poems*, but it was largely ignored until the 18th century when its Spenserian imagery came back into fashion. You can see how the introduction shifts to the alexandrine in the final line of the otherwise traditional rime royal stanza:

This is the month, and this the happy morn,
  Wherein the Son of Heav'n's eternal King,
Of wedded Maid, and Virgin Mother born,
  Our great redemption from above did bring;
  For so the holy sages once did sing,
    That he our deadly forfeit should release,
    And with his Father work us a perpetual peace.

Despite the rime royal falling out of favor during the 17th century, poets continued to dabble with heptastich constructions. In the 18th century, William Wordsworth (1770-1850) composed his "Resolution and Independence" in 20 regular rime royal stanzas. The poem opens with this:

There was a roaring in the wind all night;
The rain came heavily and fell in floods;
But now the sun is rising calm and bright;
The birds are singing in the distant woods;
Over his own sweet voice the Stock-dove broods;
The Jay makes answer as the Magpie chatters;
And all the air is filled with pleasant noise of waters.

Over time, poets began taking more liberties with the iambic pentameter *ababbcc* conventions and experimenting with other seven-line variations. Some of those forms are purely syllabic, while others require alternative rhyme schemes, alliteration, a specific theme, emphasis on particular parts of speech or letters of the alphabet, and other parameters. George Gordon, Lord Byron (1788-1824), for example, maintained the iambic pentameter tradition, but employed a new *aabccbb* rhyme scheme (since referred to as a Byron septet) in his poem, "Remembrance":

'Tis done!—I saw it in my dreams;
No more with Hope the future beams;
My days of happiness are few:
Chill'd by misfortune's wintry blast,
My dawn of life is overcast;
Love Hope, and Joy, alike adieu!
Would I could add Remembrance too!

Edgar Allan Poe (1809-1859) wrote one of the six stanzas of "Annabel Lee" as an unmetered heptastich, using an original *abbabxb* rhyme scheme:

But our love it was stronger by far than the love
Of those who were older than we,
Of many far wiser than we,
And neither the angels in heaven above,
Nor the demons down under the sea,
Can ever dissever my soul from the soul
Of the beautiful Annabel Lee.

Poe also wrote a septet called "To Margaret" that included references to Milton, Cowper, Shakespeare and Pope:

Who hath seduced thee to this foul revolt
　　From the pure well of Beauty undefiled?
　　So banished from true wisdom to prefer
　　Such squalid wit to honourable rhyme?
　　To write? To scribble? Nonsense and no more?
　　I will not write upon this argument
　　To write is human—not to write divine.

Emily Dickinson (1830-1886) penned her septet "If I Can Stop One Heart from Breaking" using an irregular meter and a novel rhyme scheme of *ababccb*:

If I can stop one heart from breaking,
I shall not live in vain;
If I can ease one life the aching,
Or cool one pain,
Or help one fainting robin
Unto his nest again,
I shall not live in vain.

Oliver Wendell Holmes (1841-1935) wrote his five-stanza "The Chambered Nautilus" in an *aabbbcc* hybrid, with each stanza mixing pentameter, trimeter and hexameter rhythms in varying line lengths. Here is the stanza number one:

This is the ship of pearl, which, poets feign,
Sails the unshadowed main,—
The venturous bark that flings
On the sweet summer wind its purpled wings
In gulfs enchanted, where the Siren sings,
And coral reefs lie bare,
Where the cold sea-maids rise to sun their streaming hair.

Laurence Binyon (1869-1943) created his own heptastich variation in his "O World, Be Nobler," an envelope verse form composed in iambic tetrameter with a rhyme scheme *AbccbaA* in which line 1 is repeated as line 7:

O World, be nobler, for her sake!
If she but knew thee what thou art,
What wrongs are borne, what deeds are done
In thee, beneath thy daily sun,
Know'st thou not that her tender heart
For pain and very shame would break?
O World, be nobler, for her sake!

Franz Werfel (1890–1945) did away with any metrical or rhyming considerations when he ventured into free-verse territory with his "Six Septets To Honor the Spring of 1905." It opens like this:

Maria Immisch was the springtime.
With feeling and reverence
I snatch her adored name from the underworld.
When I was fifteen in '05, that year
—they celebrated the big Schiller centennial
—and I saw her as heroine in his famous plays.
To this day my heart's still thankful.

J.R.R. Tolkien (1892-1973) included a seven-line song called "All Woods Must Fail" in *The Fellowship of the Ring,* the first novel in *The Lord of the Rings* trilogy. The lines follow a simple rhyme scheme of *aabbccd* and have a similar length, with either eight or nine syllables per line:

O! Wanderers in the shadowed land
Despair not! For though dark they stand,
All woods there be must end at last,
And see the open sun go past:
The setting sun, the rising sun,
The day's end, or the day begun.
For east or west all woods must fail.

The seven-line format has enjoyed a modest renaissance in the late 20th and early 21st centuries, with a bevy of newly minted forms bearing inventive names such as the alliterisen, epulaeryu, lyrette, sestonelle, seguidilla and Kwansaba.

The sevenling has become particularly popular in recent years. It is a heptastich with a similar structure to "He Loved Three Things Alone" by Anna Akhmatova (1889-1966):

He loved three things alone:
White peacocks, evensong,
Old maps of America.
He hated children crying,
And raspberry jam with his tea,
And womanish hysteria.
… And he married me.

Richard Garcia's "Five Sevens" is comprised of five
sevenlings, although he does not arrange his "sevens" in the
proscribed structure of two three-line stanzas and a single
concluding line. Here's the first stanza:

A black tablecloth billowed from a black ceiling.
An army surplus bomb casing painted black.
A night parade, seven grocery carts.
Chance reunion, a purse held upside down in Mexico City.
Screaming at La Plaza de Garibaldi.
Followed by thieves, changing cabs.
Living on the beach, pavement sways like the sea.

Sherman Alexie has also written a number of sevenlings.
"Communion" is one of my favorites:

This is the last poem I will write about salmon,
My tribe's Jesus fish, our God fish, bedamning
And bedamned. I will no longer examine

And reexamine the sins that doomed our fish.
I will not weep. My pain and fear are banished.
This is my last lamentation, my last wish:

Let my people's famine become our Eucharist.

These examples are testimony to the enduring appeal of the various heptastich forms, and new variations are being invented all the time. I have added to the contemporary canon by creating two new forms of my own, the Flint (see "Watching Koi") and the septorale ("Sixteenth Day of Spring").

A COMPENDIUM
OF SEVEN-LINE FORMS

Alliterisen
- 7 syllables per line
- rhyme scheme: *aabbccd*
- must have one alliteration per line
- could consist of 2 stanzas (Double Rhyming Alliterisen), 3 stanzas (Triple Rhyming Alliterisen), etc.
- created by Udit Bhatia

Anna
- theme: love
- unrhymed
- metric, iambic: L1 dimeter, L2 trimeter, L3 tetrameter, L4 pentameter, L5 tetrameter, L6 trimeter, L7 dimeter
- created by James R. Gray in honor of Arkansas poet and news columnist Anna Nash Yarbrough

Binyon
- an envelope verse form with refrain patterned after the poem "O World, Be Nobler" by 19th century English poet Laurence Binyon
- metric, iambic tetrameter
- rhyme scheme *AbccbaA*
- composed with a refrain; L1 is repeated as L7

Byron's Septet
* based on Lord Byron's poem "Remembrance":

> 'Tis done!—I saw it in my dreams;
> No more with Hope the future beams;
> My days of happiness are few:
> Chill'd by misfortune's wintry blast,
> My dawn of life is overcast;
> Love Hope, and Joy, alike adieu!
> Would I could add Remembrance too!

* metric, iambic tetrameter
* rhyme scheme: *aabccbb*

Cadence
* syllabic pattern: 1,2,3,4,4,8,5
* unrhymed
* created by Ella Cunningham

California Rhyme Stanza
* isosyllabic (same number of syllables each line)
* stanzaic, any number of septets
* rhyme scheme: *ababcbc*
* meter optional
* created by Barbara Dilworth and introduced at VoleCentral

Cameo
* syllabic: 2,5,8,3,8,7,2

Canopus
* metric: iambic pentameter
* rhyme scheme: *ababcbc*
* stresses a "continuous flow of thought"

- attributed to author Clement Wood of *The Complete Rhyming Dictionary and Poet's Craft Book* (1936)

Clarity Pyramid

- should be centered on the page to create a pyramid shape
- consists of 2 tercets and a lone final line
- L1: 1 syllable, the poem title, displayed in UPPER CASE
- L2: 2 syllables, a synonym of the title or a word that clarifies the title
- L3: 3 syllables, the same content as line 2
- L4,5,&6: 5, 6, and 7 syllables, and based around a life event contained within the first three lines which helps give a poetic view or outlook on the first line
- L7: 8 syllables, enclosed in quotation marks; a quotation that defines the title
- created by Jerry P. Quinn

Cross Limerick

- an American variation of the limerick, found in *Pathways of a Poet* by Viola Berg
- light verse, best used for witty, whimsical, bawdy themes
- rhyme scheme: *aabcbca*
- no title is used
- metered, in anapestic patterns: L1,2&7 are trimeter; L3,4,5&6 are dimeter

Diamante

- contrast poem set up in a diamond shape:
- L1: Noun or subject
  L2: 2 Adjectives describing the first noun/subject
  L3: 3 -ing words describing the first noun/subject
  L4: 4 words: 2 about the first noun/subject, 2 about the antonym/synonym
  L5: 3 -ing words about the antonym/synonym

L6: 2 adjectives describing the antonym/synonym
L7: Antonym/synonym for the subject

Duni

- metric:
  L1: one dactyl followed by 2 trochees and an Iamb
  L2: 3 iambs
  L3: one trochee followed by an anapest and 2 iambs
  L4: 3 iambs
  L5: 3 iambs
  L6: 4 iambs (includes a pivot or change of thought)
  L7: one iamb, followed by an anapest and an iamb
- rhyme scheme: *abcacba*
- created by Mildred Dewey

Duodora

- a quatorzain (14-line poem) that doesn't claim to be a sonnet
- written in 2 septets: L1 of the first septet is repeated as L1 of the second septet
- syllabic pattern: 4,6,5,5,5,10,10 / 4,6,5,5,5,10,10
- rhymed Axxxxxb, Axxxxxb, L1 is repeated as a refrain that begins the second stanza (x is unrhymed)
- created by Dora Tompkins

Epulaeryu

- theme: delicious food
- rhymed or unrhymed
- 33 syllables: 7,5,7,5,5,3,1
- each line has a thought about the main course
- L7 expresses the writer's feelings about the food
- ends with an exclamation point
- created by Joseph Spence, Sr.

Flint

- theme: water
- rhyme scheme: *abcaacb*
- syllable pattern: 8,8,10,8,10,8,10
- uses Flint, Michigan's area code (810) as basis for its syllable pattern
- created by Wayne Lee in memory of the Flint Water Crisis of 2016

Kwansaba

- a praise poem developed in 1995 by Eugene B Redmond in honor of Kwanzaa, the 7-day celebration of African-American family, culture, heritage and principles
- adopts the number 7 from Kwanzaa's Nguzo Saba (7 principles of unity, self- determination, collective work and responsibility, cooperative economics, purpose, creativity, and faith)
- name derived from Swahili *kwan* ("first fruit") and *saba* ("principle")
- 7 words in each line, with no word exceeding 7 letters

Lancaster

- 2 stanzas of 7 lines each
- rhyme scheme: *aba(c)(b)dd, efe(c)(f)gg*
- the lines in parentheses end in half-rhymes

Lyrette

- syllabic pattern: 2,3,4,5,4,3,2
- unrhymed
- created by Dr. Israel Newman

Neville

- metric: L1,4&7 are iambic tetrameter; L2,3,5&6 are iambic trimeter
- rhyme scheme: *abbacca*

Pleiades
- all 7 lines start with same letter as the title
- only one word is allowed in the title, followed by a single 7-line stanza
- any meter
- created in 1999 by Craig Tigerman
- Hortensia Anderson added her own requirement of restricting the line length to 6 syllables

Pyramid
- shaped like a pyramid, with one word on the top line, then adding a word on each successive line
- no requirements for rhyme, syllable count or rhythmic patterns
- can be inverted, starting with 7 words in the first line

Rime royal (Rhyme royal, Rhyme royal stanza, Troilus stanza, Chaucerian stanza)
- flexible verse, can be written as lyrical, narrative, commentary or literary burlesque
- often written in iambic pentameter, but was originally simply decasyllabic
- stanzaic, written in any number of septets
- rhyme scheme: *ababbcc*
- can be composed either as a tercet and 2 couplets (*aba bb cc*) or as a quatrain followed by a tercet (*abab bcc*)
- pioneered by Geoffrey Chaucer

Saraband
- Spanish (rhyme scheme: *axa bcbc*)
- Italian (rhyme scheme: *aaa bccb*)
- French (rhyme scheme: *axa bbbc*)
- taken from the musical 16th century Saraband dance form, which has an alternate meter of 3-4
- 2 stanzas: a tercet followed by a quatrain

- in the tercet all 3 lines might or might not rhyme
- can mix rhyme scheme of quatrains, e.g., Spanish with French or Italian, when writing long poems

Seafonn
- Anglo Saxon for "seven"
- made up of a quintain followed by a couplet
- rhyme scheme: *abccb aa*
- an argument is presented in the first 5 lines and the counterpoint in the ending couplet
- metric: iambic tetrameter, with L2&5 catalectic (metrically incomplete; lacking part of the last foot)
- introduced by Elizabeth Maxwell Phelps

Seguidilla
- began as a popular dance song of Spain and branched into variations by the 17th century
- alternating long short rhythm
- stanzaic, written in any number of 2-part septets
- syllabic pattern: 7,5,7,5 / 5,7,5 with a slight pause between L4 and L5 suggesting L4 should be end-stopped
- rhymed by assonance *xaxabxb* or *xaxabab*, x being unrhymed (true rhyme is generally not used)
- composed with a volta or change in thought between L4 and L5
- sometimes serves as a conclusion for another verse

Sept
- syllable count starts at one in L1, increasing by one each line up to L4, then decreasing at the same rate until L7 has one syllable again (1,2,3,4,3,2,1)

Septet
- blank verse, free verse or any meter
- rhyme scheme: *aabbccx*

Septet II
- an English form with syllabic pattern: 3,5,7,9,7,5,3

Septolet
- contains 14 words with a break in between the 2 parts
- both parts deal with the same idea

Septanelle
- syllabic: 4,6,10,4,6,10,4
- rhyme scheme: *ababcca*

Septorale
- theme: nature-based
- rhyme scheme: *aabcacb*
- no syllabic requirements
- created by Wayne Lee

Sevenling
- created by Roddy Lumsden, based on Anna Akhmatova's "He Loved Three Things Alone":

> He loved three things alone:
> White peacocks, evensong,
> Old maps of America.
> He hated children crying,
> And raspberry jam with his tea,
> And womanish hysteria.
> … And he married me.

- divides the poem into 2 tercets, with a lone L7
- like Akhmatova's poem, the form uses 2 sets of 3 elements—objects, statements, actions, situations, possibilities, etc.–which can be connected directly, indirectly or not at all

- the tagline draws both tercets together in surprising, often mysterious ways
- no fixed syllable count, meter or rhyme pattern

Shanzi
- syllabic: 4,5/ 5,4/ 4,4,5
- 2 couplets and a tercet
- unrhymed

Sicilian Septet
- rhyme scheme: *abababa*
- no set form; later iambic

Spanish Septet (Septilla)
- rhyme scheme: *aabccba*
- no set form; later Iambic

Star Sevlin
- a shape poem that is supposed to form a star when centered on the page
- iambic, 4,6,8,6,8,6,4 syllables per line
- rhyme scheme: *abbcaca*
- created by Lilliann Mathilda Svenson, based on poems found in *Pathways of a Poet* by Viola Berg

Swinburne
- stanzaic form patterned after "Before the Mirror" by Algernon Charles Swinburne (1837-1909), first stanza of which is:

      White rose in red rose-garden
      Is not so white;
      Snowdrops that plead for pardon
      And pine for fright
      Because the hard East blows

Over their maiden rows
Grow not as this face grows from pale to bright.

- written in any number of septets
- metric: L1,3,5&6 are trimeter; L2&4 are dimeter; L7 is pentameter
- L1&3 have feminine or falling rhyme
- rhyme scheme: *ababcc b, dedeff e*, etc.

Trinet
- stanzaic: written in any number of septets (3 are recommended)
- measured in words rather than syllables or metric feet: 2,2,6,6,2,2,2 words in each line
- should be centered on the page to appear as crosses
- unrhymed
- created by *zion*

Whitney
- syllable pattern: 3,4,3,4,3,4,7

Thanks to Harvard University, poetry.com, thepoetsgarret.com, poetrybase.info, Judi Van Gorder (poetrymagnumopus.com), Viola Berg, poetscollective.org, dversepoets.com, poetscollective. org, poetrybase.info and popularpoetryforms.com, from which I compiled much of this information.

ACKNOWLEDGMENTS

My thanks to the editors of the publications where the following poems previously appeared, sometimes in alternate versions:

Abandoned Mine: "Survivor"; *A Wind Blows Through Us: A Festival of New Mexico Men's Poetry:* "Apricots"; *Bombfire:* "A Walk with My Mother"; *Buddha's Cat:* "Three-Legged Dog"; *Discretionary Love*: "What a Wonderful World"; *Eunoia Review:* "Windowpane" and "Sixteenth Day of Spring: A Septorale"; *Fixed & Free Anthology 2021:* "Friend," "An Elder Addresses His Pain," "Root Soup," "Echo Amphitheater" and "The Keening"; *Heimat Review:* "Esme"; *Kahini Quarterly:* "Wild Goose," "Her Brushes, Her Pens, Her" and "Navigator"; *Minnow Literary Magazine:* "Wildfires"; *Leaping Clear:* "A Bit Like Lilacs: A Rime Royale," "A Word from Grandmother" and "Minor Deities"; *Poems from County Clare and Far Beyond: An anthology of Irish poets and friends around the world:* "Dining on Salt: A Whitney" and "Hot: A Sept"; *We Don't Break, We Burn: Poems of Resiliency:* "Kumbhaka" and "Spring, again"; *Where Flowers Bloom—Poems and Essays of Strength, Hope, and Resilience:* "Flying"; *Writer's Digest:* "Reading to My Wife" and "What Lies Within: A Spanish Septet"; *Zingara Poetry Review:* "The Lark Ascended"

* * *

I'm deeply grateful to my family, friends, colleagues, therapists, men's group, and late wife Alice Rose Lee for their ongoing support while researching, writing, and editing this book. Special thanks to my new life partner Mary Rives, who stood by me every step of the way during my writing and grieving processes. Mary served unselfishly as my first reader, best listener, and constant source of comfort, compassion, and encouragement.

I'm also grateful to colleagues Lauren Camp, Alicia Hokanson, John Macker, David Meischen, Mary McGinnis, and Hiram Larew for their support and encouragement.

Last but not least, thank you to Cornerstone Press Director & Publisher Dr. Ross K. Tangedal and his staff, including editorial director Brett Hill, cover desginer Samantha Bjork, media director Ava Willett, sales director Sophie McPherson, and sales managers Madison Schultz and Autumn Vine for their unwavering patience, persistence, and professionalism.

WAYNE LEE is a writer, editor and teacher. Lee's poems have appeared in *Tupelo Press, Slipstream, The New Guard, The Lowestoft Chronicle, Writer's Digest,* and other journals and anthologies. He was awarded the 2012 Fischer Prize and has been nominated for a Pushcart Prize and four Best of the Net Awards. His collection *The Underside of Light* was a finalist for the 2014 New Mexico/Arizona Book Award. His chapbook *Buddha's Cat* was published in May 2024. Lee is the founder and host of the online Tuesday Poetry Practice community. He lives in Santa Fe, New Mexico.